BOWLING GAMES

A New Twist on Your Favorite Sport

Table of Contents

    I. Introduction

    II. Items Needed and Suggested Game Levels

    III. Games

1.	Baseball	11.	Tic Tac Toe
2.	Phone Number Game	12.	Football
3.	Boxing	13.	Streaker
4.	Perfect 992	14.	Card Pull
5.	Poker	15.	9 Pin Knockout
6.	Golf	16.	Lucky Roll Race
7	Score is Right or Hit Your Average	17.	Badges
8.	Darts	18.	Bingo
9.	Knockout	19.	Brackets
10.	Thirst Quencher	20.	Blackjack

    IV. Game Sheets

    V. Glossary

Introduction

This book is designed to be used by a bowler of any skill level. As a training tool or just for some additional fun to your games, the games presented in this book will be useful whether you bowl once a year or seven days a week. Many of these games can be played if you are just bowling a practice game by yourself or bowling with a group. While some games are tailored towards bowlers of a higher skill level, most games can be adjusted to fit the skill level of all the bowlers. Like any competition, games are usually better when the competition level of all involved is nearly equal. However, it may be necessary at times to adjust a game so that one bowler is bound by the more advanced rules while other bowlers are utilizing the least advanced option of the game. In many instances the options will be explained within the game itself; however, sometimes you may need to improvise as appropriate.

If you are already a scratch bowler, you may be wondering how these games can benefit you. Conversely, if you are new to bowling, or if your skills are a bit rusty, you may be wondering if these games will prove to be too challenging. However, the challenges of bowling a specific number of pins when required can help you heighten and control your skills if you are at a higher level of bowling ability, or to learn the basics of control and precision of your shots if you are not yet a scratch bowler. Not only are these games a great way to improve and learn skills, they add a fun challenge to a game that may have become mere routine for the scratch bowler, and provide an interesting training tool for the beginner.

The games may also help level the playing field between bowlers of different caliber. For example, the recreational bowler in a traditional bowling game may try to get a strike and only get a five, in which case he would soon be left behind by the scratch bowler. However, if playing a game in which the goal is to bowl a five, the more accomplished bowler may struggle for this result in much the same way that the beginner struggled to bowl a strike. Again these games can be used as training guides or just too simply add a new splash of life to the traditional game of bowling. We hope you find the games interesting and challenging, and we wish you the best of luck in all your bowling endeavors.

Common Terms and Basic Explanations

A few of the basic terms of bowling and some explanation of essential information that will be referenced in the games.

Pins

Bowling pins are initially set up in the same order as shown below. Each pin is assigned a number 1-10 based on its starting position. These pins retain their initial pin number, no matter where they may end up after the first ball is thrown. For example, if you roll the ball and knock all the pins down, except the 5 pin, but the 5 pin slides and stands where the 6 pin initially began, that pin is still the 5 pin. This is a rare occurrence, but from time to time it does occur. The more common scenario is that a bowler will bowl and leave 1 or more pins standing. So, if the bowler leaves the 7 and the 10 pin standing after the first throw, someone may say they have a 7-10 (referring to the number of the pins that remain standing) split.

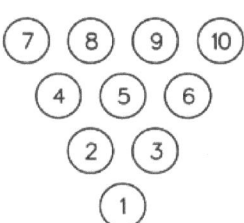

Bowling Terms

- **Convert** – This is another way to state the bowler has picked-up a spare or a split.

- **First Throw** – This is the first throw in any particular frame.

- **Frame** – The typical game of bowling consists of 10 frames. Each frame consists of the bowler's chance to knock down all 10 pins using one or two throws.

- **Handicap** – These are additional points awarded to a bowler to help level the field among bowlers with different skill levels. For example, a base score of 200 may be established and if a bowler has an average of 150, the handicap is 50. If the bowler bowls a scratch game of 170, then with his or her handicap, their score would be 220.

- **Open Frame** - An open frame is any frame in which a bowler fails to knock down all 10 pins in the 2 throws allotted for the particular frame.

- **Pick-up** – This is another name for a spare.

- **Scratch Game** – This refers to a game bowled with no handicap added.

- Spare – A spare is obtained when all 10 pins are knocked down by a bowler in one frame using two throws.

- Split – A split, as referred to in this book, means any situation wherein the pins left standing after the first throw meet these criteria:
  1) More than 1 pin standing;
  2) The head pin, or "1" pin, is not left standing; and
  3) The pins left standing have had at least one pin between them knocked down
  4) Splits are typically designated on automatic scoring machines by denoting the number of pins in red or by circling the number. In this book, when splits are used for examples, they will be denoted as the number with a circle around it.

- Split Conversion - This refers to any situation where the bowler bowls a split and knocks down all the remaining pins on the next turn.

- Strike – A strike is obtained when all 10 pins are knocked down by a bowler in one frame using one throw.

- Tenth Frame – The tenth frame is the bowler's final frame in a game. The tenth differs from all other frames in that if a bowler rolls a strike in his or her first throw in this frame, he or she earns two additional throws. If the bowler does not strike on the first throw, but obtains a spare in the second throw, then they earn one additional throw.

Items Needed

Many games will only require a pen and paper (and maybe a calculator for some of you), but some games will need additional items. If you are unsure which games you might play, you may wish to have all these items available.
- Deck(s) of Playing Cards
- Dice
- Pen and Paper
- Money

Suggested Game Levels

All the games can be adjusted to be used by the beginner bowler and/or the most advanced bowler. Each game has a suggested level presented as to who the game is best tailored for. These are just suggested levels.

    <u>Beginner</u> Those who are just beginning the game of bowling or who bowl infrequently.
    <u>Intermediate</u> Those who bowl fairly regularly but are not yet scratch bowlers.
    <u>Advanced</u> Those who bowl regularly and have a 160 or above average.

The rules of each game can be adjusted from time to time to meet the needs of the group. Just be sure you all agree on the changes before the game begins.

Game 1: Bowling Baseball

Suggested level: Intermediate to Advanced Bowlers

Items Needed: Pen and paper. A knowledge of the rules of baseball are also needed. This game is not suggested for bowlers who do not under the basic rules of baseball.

Object of the Game: Score more runs than your opponent in 9 innings, or if you wish to abbreviate the game to a certain number of frames, the bowler with the most runs in the fewest number of innings wins. Bowlers are awarded bases on the number of pins knocked down after the first throw.

Rules:

1) Determine how many frames (remember there are 10 frames per game) of bowling will be used in this baseball game.
2) Each bowler bowls his or her game independent of the other bowlers, so it is possible in 10 frames of bowling, one bowler may have completed 1 inning and another bowler completed 2 innings.
3) Determine the scoring conversion system, a suggested scoring system is set forth in Rule #4.
4) The suggested scoring is as follows:
   a. 5 Pins = HR
   b. 6 Pins = 3B
   c. 7 Pins = 2B
   d. 8 Pins = 1B

   ** A bowler is only awarded bases based on the first throw. For example, a bowler who bowls a 4 in the first roll earns an out for that roll, if they bowl a 1 in the second throw they earn another out (failure to convert a spare – See Rule #5) and not a HR.
5) All other pin counts are outs, but a bowling strike (ten pins in one throw) counts as two (2) outs.
6) Any open frame (i.e. the bowler does not knock down 10 pins in the frame's 2 throws), then the bowler has made an out.
7) Once a bowler makes three outs, all base runners are removed from the bases and an inning is concluded for that bowler only.
8) If the bowler rolls a split, and then converts the split then all runners advance one extra base.
9) You must keep track of the position of all runners in any given inning. After each frame your runners are repositioned after your first throw, and in some occasions after your second throw.
10) All runners already on base advance the number of bases that the hitter, this being the person who rolled, advanced.

Sample Scoring:

If this game was played as the entire game this bowler would have played 2 2/3 innings and scored 3 runs.
In this example, the baseball equivalent is stated in **red**.

Frame	1	2	3	4	5	6	7	8	9	10
1st Roll	7 **(2B)**	X **(2 outs)**	8 **(1B)**	7 **(2B)**	4 **(out)**	8 **(1B)**	5 **(HR)**	6 **(3B)**	8 – split **(1B)**	4 **(out)**|8 **(1B)**
2nd Roll	2 **(out)**	--	/	/	5 **(out)**	1 **(out)**	4 **(out)**	/	/	/
Position of base runners	Runner on 2nd, 1 out	Strike = 2 outs. 3 outs and inning is over.	Runner on 1st, no outs	Runner on 1st advances 2 bases. Runners on 2nd and 3rd.	2 Outs. Runners do not advance.	Runner on 3rd scores. 1 Run, 3 outs and inning is over.	Home Run. One run scores and one out.	Runner on third.	Runner on 3rd scores, batter goes to first, then to 2nd because the spare was picked up.	Single moves the runner to third.

Game 2: Phone Number Game

Suggested level: Intermediate to Advanced Bowers.

Items Needed: Pen and paper

Object of the Game: A phone number, or any other 10 digit number, is selected at the beginning of the game. The first digit of the 10 digit number is assigned to the first frame, the second number to the second frame, and so on. The bowlers then try to bowl the designated number for the selected frame to "earn that number".

The person with the highest score, which is calculated by taking the bowlers traditional bowling score and multiplying it times the multiplier earned, is the winner.

Rules:

1) Select a phone number or other 10 digit number.
2) Begin bowling. If the bowler bowls a number of pins equal to the assigned digit for that frame (see below for additional details), they earn that number.
3) A 0 is earned by bowling a strike.
4) No number is earned for a double gutter.
5) If the bowler bowls the designated number on the first throw then they are given credit for obtaining the number. If they do not get the number on the first throw, then, if possible, they may try to get that number on the second throw. For example, if the number is 8, and the bowler rolls an 8 on the first throw, then they are given credit for rolling the 8, whether or not they pick up the spare. If they roll 6 on the first throw, they can try and get 2 of the remaining pins to get credit for bowling the designated number.
6) If the number is 3 and the bowler bowls a 4 on the first throw, they cannot earn the number, even if they bowl a 3 on the second throw. Numbers can only be earned on the first throw or the combination of the 2 throws for one frame.
7) A bowler can have up to 3 attempts to get the number in the final frame. For example, if the last number is a 9 and a bowler bowls 2 strikes and a 9, then they get credit for earning the number.
8) At the end of the game, each bowler takes their traditional bowling score and multiplies it by the earned multiplier.
9) The bowler with the highest score (Traditional bowling score x the earned multiplier) wins.

Multipliers:

0 Numbers = No multiplier

1 Number = Multiplier of 1.5

2 or more = Multiplier equal to number of digits bowled.

Sample Scoring:

Using the phone number / designated number of 6148675309, you might have the sample scoring below:

Frame	1	2	3	4	5	6	7	8	9	10
Designated Number	6	1	4	8	6	7	5	3	0	9
Traditional Bowling Score	6 / 12	2 6 20	3 1 34	7 2 43	5 2 50	7 2 59	6 / 73	4 / 92	9 / 110	8 / 9 129
# Earned	Yes	No	Yes	No	No	Yes	No	No	No	Yes

Final Score = 129 x 4 (one for each yes) = 516

Game 3: Boxing

Suggested Level: Any

Items Needed: Pen and paper

Object of the Game: Bowl against your opponent in a "boxing match" not to exceed 10 rounds and try to "knock them out", win more rounds than they win, or score more points than they do.

Rules:

1) Select 2 Bowlers who will bowl head to head.
2) After each frame, the bowler with the highest number of total pins knocked down in the frame is awarded the frame.
3) If each bowler knocks down the same number of pins, the frame is a draw and no one wins the round.
a. For purposes of this game, spare of any kind is 10 pins. So, a 3 spare and 9 spare are equal. A strike is greater than a spare.
4) If a bowler bowls a strike and their opponent does not, then they not only win the round, but score a knock down as well.
5) A bowler that first earns 3 knock downs in any game wins by knock out.
6) If no bowler obtains a knockout, then the bowler who wins the most rounds wins the game.
7) If the bowlers win the same number of rounds, then the bowler with the highest score wins the game.
8) In the 10th frame a bowler can only win the frame once, meaning only one point is awarded for that round, however, a player can obtain up to three knock downs if they bowl 3 strikes in a row and their opponent fails to bowl a strike.
9) The winner of the 10th frame is determined by the bowler with the highest last roll if the bowlers both throw an equal number of throws.

Sample Scoring:

The highlighted frame indicates the winner for the round. 🥊 Indicates a total knock downs.

Frame	1	2	3	4	5	6	7	8	9	10
Bowler #1	6 / 20	X 39	4 5 48	8 / 64	6 3 73	7 / 93	X 122	X 141	9 - 150	9 / X 170
Bowler #2	7 / 19	9 / 38	9 - 47	7 2 56	5 / 76	X 96	6 / 116	X 136	9 / 154	8 / 9 173

In the above example, Bowler #1 wins via a Knock out in the 10th frame. Bowler #1 would have also won by points, as he won 4 rounds to Bowler #2's 3 rounds; however, if the game had come down to the third tie breaker (the overall highest score), Bowler #2 would have won 173-170.

Game 4: Perfect 992

Suggested Level: Any

Items Needed: None, Pen and paper may be needed.

Object of the Game: The bowler with the highest reversed score (after applying adjustments, if necessary) at the end of standard 10 frame game of bowling wins.

Rules:
1) Each bowler bowls a complete game of bowling (10 frames).
2) If a bowler bowls two gutter balls in one frame, or a gutter ball in the tenth frame in the throw after a spare or two strikes, then the number of pins thrown by the next bowler on his first throw is deducted from the player's score, except that if the bowler throwing the gutter ball(s) is the last bowler, in which case the first ball thrown by the previous bowler is used to deduct from the final score.
3) If the bowler's score used as a deduction is a strike, that bowler may choose, at that time, the amount of pins, up to 9, to be deducted from the final score.
4) At the end of the game, each bowlers score is reversed and the bowler with the highest score wins.

Examples:
Bowler 1 bowls a 170
Bowler 2 bowls a 166
Bowler 3 bowls a 107
Bowler 4 bowls a 117

The winner in the game is Bowler 4, as their score is 711, Bowler 3 scored a 701, Bowler 2 scored a 661 and Bowler 1 scored a 71.

Game 5: Poker

Suggested Level: Any

Items Needed: Deck(s) of Cards

Object of the Game: Obtain the best possible Poker hand

Rules:

1) Each player contributes a designated amount to the pot as a buy in.
2) If a player bowls a strike, then the player draw 2 cards from anywhere in the deck.
3) If the player bowls a spare, then they draw 1 card from the deck.
4) Any other rolls result in no cards drawn.
5) At the conclusion of the game, the player with the best 5-card poker hand wins the game and the pot.

Variation:
Players can only hold up to 8 cards at a time. If the player rolls a strike or spare and wish to draw another card, they may do so, but must discard a card or cards after drawing from the deck, so the player at no time hold more than 8 cards. Discarded cards may not be redrawn.

Game 6: Golf

Suggested Level: Any

Items Needed: Pen and paper. A basic understanding of golf is also needed for this game.

Object of the Game: Similar to the traditional game of golf, the player with the lowest golf score wins this game.

Rules:

1) Establish Par for each hole
2) Establish a Par Base
    a. 9 or 10 is the suggested par base
        i. Any value under 10 makes it possible to score 0 or negative numbers on certain holes
3) Add the Par Base to par to get the bowling par base.
4) Bowl and subtract your score from the bowling par base to get your golf score.
    a. All open frames are worth the value bowled
    b. Spares = 10
    c. Strikes = 11
    d. Split conversions = 12
5) Determine the 10th frame options to be used.
    a. Assign a par value and play "10" holes.
    b. Allow the bowler to use it as a Mulligan for any previous hole
        i. The hole the Mulligan is being used on must be declared before bowling the 10th frame.
    c. Use the 10th frame as a tie breaker.
    d. Use as a free frame.
    e. Use the 1st frame as a practice frame.
6) The bowler with the highest actual bowling score will be declared the winner in the event of tied golf score.

Example:
10th frame free option with 10 as the par base.

Frame	1	2	3	4	5	6	7	8	9	10
Par	4	3	4	5	4	4	3	5	4	--
Bowling Base Score (add 10 to par)	14	13	14	15	14	14	13	15	14	--
Bowling Score	9 / 19	9 - 28	⑧1 37	X 57	⑦/ 73	6 2 81	9 / 99	8 - 107	9 / 126	9 / X 146
Golf Score	4 (14-10)	4 (13-9)	5 (14-9)	4 (15-11)	2 (14-12)	6 (14-18)	3 (13-10)	7 (15-8)	4 (14-10)	39 +3 (3 over par)

Game 7: Score is Right or Hit your Average

Suggested Level: Any

Items Needed: Pen, paper and money if desired.

Object of the Game: A score is determined at the beginning of the game and each bowler attempts to get closest to the predetermined score. The bowler closest to the predetermined score, as determined by the rules of the game, is the winner.

Rules:

1) Select a Target score for the game.
    a. If the level of the participants vary greatly, a different score may be selected for each bowler to obtain.
2) Determine the scoring and wagering structure, if any, for the game. The following structure, all or part of which may be incorporated, is suggested:
    a. $1.00 Entry Fee to enter the game.
    b. Any frame in which the bowler bowls a ball (either first or second ball) and does not hit a pin, they must contribute $0.10 to the pot. If a bowler bowls two gutter balls in one frame, then rule 2(c) is applied in place of this rule.
    c. Any frame in which the bowler does not knock down a single pin, they contributes $.25 X the frame number to the pot. For example, a double gutter in the 7th frame means the bowler contributes $1.75 to the pot (7 x $.25)
    d. Any frame in which the bowler bowls double gutters, 12 pins are added to their score for each frame where double gutters were bowled if the final score is at or above the target score and 12 pins are subtracted for each frame where double gutters were bowled if their final score is below the target score.
        i. This is done to prevent a player from "sitting" on a score.
    e. If a Player obtains and converts a split, every other player pays that player $.50.
    f. At the end of the game, each bowler must contribute an additional $.10 per pin, for each pin their adjusted score is less than the target score.
    g. At the end of the game, each bowler must contribute an additional $.25 per pin, for each pin their adjusted score is more than the target score.
    h. At the end of the game, the person closest to the target score (after adjustments) wins the pot. In the event of a tie, the player(s) who were closest without going over win/split the pot.
    i. If one person(s) obtains the target score perfectly, every other player must contribute an extra $1.00 to the pot.

Example:

The target score is **142**.

Player 1 bowls a 147 – They are 5 pins over and must contribute $1.00 (Entry Fee) + $1.25 ($.25 for each pin over 142) for a total of $2.25.

Player 2 bowls a 143, but bowled a double gutter in the 9th frame – They are 1 pin over on the raw score, but with the 12 pin adjustment their adjusted score is 155 and they are 13 pins over the target score. They must contribute $1.00 + $3.25 ($.25 per each pin over 142) + $2.25 for a double gutter in the 9th for a total of $6.50.

Player 3 bowls a 137, but bowled a 9 gutter, 6 gutter, and 8 gutter in their game. They are 5 pins under and must contribute $1.00 + $0.30 (3 gutters x $.10) + $.50 ($.10 for each pin under the target score) for a total of $1.80

Player 4 bowls a 135 – They owe $1.00 + $.70 ($.70 for each pin under the target score) for a total of $1.70.

In this game the final pot was $12.25 and Player 3 won the pot. The final standings were:
- Player 3 = - 5
- Player 4 = -7
- Player 2 = +13
- Player 1 = +17

Game 8: Darts

Suggested Level: Any

Items Needed: Pen and paper.

Object of the Game: This game is an abbreviated version of point cricket in darts. The game can be contracted or expanded based on the anticipated number of games bowled.

Rules:

1) Select 3 outcomes as your targets for the game. The suggested outcomes are:
   a. Strike
   b. 9 /
   c. 8 /
2) Each bowler bowls and tries to obtain one of the target scores.
3) If one player obtains the target score twice, before the other player obtains the target score twice then they earn points for each target score they obtain before the final player has obtained two of the target value scores.
4) The player with the most points at the end wins.

	Bowler 1		Bowler 2	
X	Marked as Completed	Points	Marked as Completed	Points
9 /				
8 /				

Game 9: Knockout

Suggested Level: Intermediate to Advanced

Items Needed: Pen and paper.

Object of the Game: Obtain the highest score using bonus points.

Rules:

1) There are two variations to this game. In the first variation, in order to earn the bonus points a player must bowl the designated number (as explained below) and convert the spare in order to earn bonus points. In the second variation, bonus points may be earned by bowling the designated number in one throw (using the first number bowled) if the spare is converted, or the combination of two throws if no spare is obtained.
2) Bonus points can only be obtained once per designated number. For example, if a bowler bowls a strike, then they earn 5 bonus points. If they bowl a second strike, they earn no bonus points.
3) If a bowler converts a split and has already obtained the designated number associated with the split, then they may select any designated number not yet obtained.
   a. For example, if a bowler bowls a 7 / and then later picks up a 7 split, then can chose any number for bonus points
4) The final score is calculated by taking the bowled score and adding the bonus points.
5) The player with the highest final score is the winner.

Example:
Using variation one.

Bonus Points	50	40	30	20	10	9	8	7	6	5
Score needed to obtain bonus	1	2	3	4	5	6	7	8	9	10 (strike)

Bowling Score	8 / 18	8 - 26	⑧1 35	X 55	6 / 67	2 6 75	3 / 94	9 - 112	8 / 125	3 / X 145
Bonus Points	7	0	0	5	9	0	30	6	0	0

The bowler's final score is 202. (145+7+5+9+30+6 Bowling Score + Bonus Points)

Game 10: Thirst Quencher

Suggested Level: Any

Items Needed: None

Object of the Game: To try to not be the only bowler who does not bowl a strike in any given frame.

Rules:

1) If a bowler fails to bowl a strike in a frame where all other bowlers bowl a strike, then that bowler must buy the rest of the bowlers a beverage of his or her choice.

Game 11: Tic Tac Toe

Suggested Level: Any

Items Needed: Pen and paper

Object of the Game: To be the first player to obtain 3 marks in a vertical, horizontal or diagonal line.

Rules:

1) Draw a 9 space grid.
2) Select who will be X and who will be O
3) If a Player strikes they may place their mark on any open space on the grid.
4) The first player to get 3 of their marks in a vertical, horizontal or diagonal line wins the game.

Game 12: Football

Suggested Level: Intermediate to Advanced

Items Needed: Pen and paper.

Object of the Game: Score the most points in accordance with the scoring system set forth in the rules.

Rules:

1) All bowlers earn points when any of the following bowling scores are earned in any one frame.
   a. 2 / = safety or 2 points
   b. 3/ = field goal or 3 points
   c. 6 - = touchdown – failed extra point or 6 points
      i. There must be a total of 6 pins for the frame. So any combination of two throws that equals 6 pins.
   d. 6 / = touchdown – extra point good or 7 points.
   e. 7/ = touchdown – extra point good or 7 points.
   f. ⑧ / = touchdown – two point conversion or 8 points.

2) Bowlers may also earn points by accumulating "yards" as follows:
   a. Any open frame, except for one equaling 6 pins, the bowler earns yards in an amount equal to the number of pins knocked down.
   b. Any spare other than the ones stated above = 10 yards
   c. Any strike = 20 yards

3) Each 80 yards = touchdown
   a. If the frame in which the 80 yards is reach is an open – then 6 points are earned
   b. If the frame in which the 80 yards is reach is a spare – then 7 points are earned
   c. If the frame in which the 80 yards is reach is a strike – then 8 points are earned
   d. If more than 80 yards are reached in a turn, the excess yards do not carry over and the player starts at 0 yards on the next turn.

4) The player with the most points wins.

Example:
Using variation one.

Frame	1	2	3	4	5	6	7	8	9	10
Bowling Score	6 / 20	X 39	4 5 48	8 / 64	6 - 70	5 / 90	X 108	8 – 116	9 – 125	7/X 145
Football Points	7 Points	0 points	0 points	0 points	6 points	0 points	0 points	0 points	6 points	7 points
Football Yards	No yards	20 yards	9 yards – total of 29 yards	10 yards – total of 39 yards	0 yards – total of 39 yards	10 yards – total of 49 yards	20 yards – 69 yards total	8 yards – 77 yards total	9 yards were earned = 86 yards, but because it was an open, only 6 points were earned	20 yards earned.

In the above example, 26 points were earned and the Bowler's score is 26

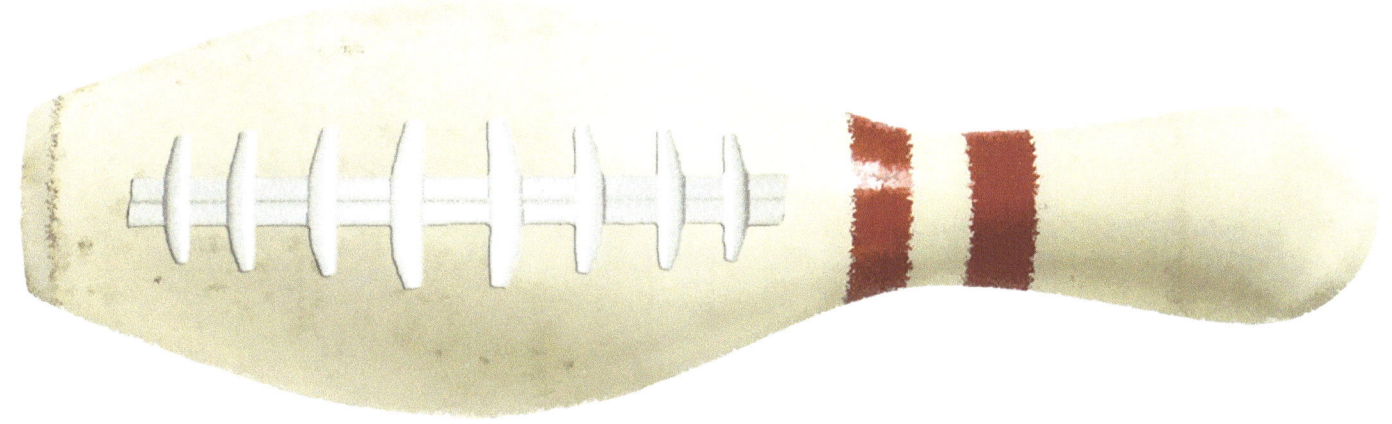

Game 13: Streaker

Suggested Level: Intermediate to Advanced

Items Needed: Pen and paper.

Object of the Game: Bowlers attempt to build a streak of first balls thrown in an up or down direction. The player who obtains the longest streak wins.

Rules:

1) Each bowler bowls the first frame.
2) After the first frame, the bowler must designate whether they want to try and obtain a streak by bowling in an upward manner or a downward manner. This designation cannot be changed after the first frame, except if the bowler bowls a 1 or a strike, then the manner changes until that streak is broken or another 1 or strike is bowled.
    a. An upward manner means that a bowler will start, for example, at 4 and try to bowl a 5, then a 6 and so on.
    b. A downward manner means that a bowler will start, for example, at a 9 and try to bowl an 8 and then a 7, and so on.
3) Even if streak is broken, the bowler must continue the same direction (upward or downward) that he was following before.
    a. If he is bowling upward and bowls a 5 and then a 7, he must try to bowl an 8 next, starting a new streak.
4) Only the number of pins knocked down in the first throw is used in the streak.
    a. For example, a 6 – is different from a 3-3, although 6 total pins were knocked down in the frame. The former counts as a 6, whereas the latter counts as a 3.
5) A streak's starting point is established by the preceding frame. So, for example, if a bowler rolls a 6 in the first ball in the first frame and then an 8 in the next first ball of the second frame, in order to start a streak in the third frame they will need to bowl a 7 or a 9, depending on the designation made in step 2.
6) If a Bowler rolls a gutter or a strike on the first ball, then next number in the streak must be a 1 or a 9. A gutter does not count as a number in the streak, so a bowler who bowls a 2-1-gutter has a streak of 1 and must start the streak over.
7) At the conclusion of the game, each bowler adds the numbers on the corresponding chart for each number in any streak and the total of those numbers is used as a multiplier.
    a. The first number in the streak does not count. For example, if a bowler is bowling in an upward manner and bowls an 8-9-8. Then the streak is 1 (8 to 9) and only the 9 is used to obtain the multiplier.
8) The bowler with the highest bowling score multiplied by the total of the earned multiplier wins.

Example:

First Throw	Multiplier
1	8
2	7
3	6
4	5
5	4
6	3
7	2
8	2
9	.5
10	.25

Bowler elected the upward option

Frame	1	2	3	4	5	6	7	8	9	10
Bowler #1	6 / 15	5 4 24	6 / 42	8 / 61	9 / 81	X 101	9 / 121	X 141	8 / 158	7 - 165
Multiplier Earned	--	--	3	--	.5	.25	.5	--	--	--

The bowlers final score is 165 x (3 + .5 + .25 + .5) or 165 x 4.25 (the total of the multipliers) = 701.25

Game 14: Card Pull

Suggested Level: Any

Items Needed: Deck of Cards

Object of the Game: Collect the most cards.

Rules:

1) Shuffle a deck of playing cards and lay them face down on a table.
2) Before bowling, each player selects a card from anywhere in the pile.
3) The bowler then attempts to bowl the value of that card in the first throw or a combination of two throws.
   a. Cards values are 1 (Ace) – 9 = the number of pins required.
   b. A card with a value of 10 = a spare
   c. A face card = a strike
4) For example, if the bowler draws a 3 and bowls a 2 on the first throw, they must bowl a 1 on the second throw in order to earn the card. If the bowler bowls a 3 on the first throw, then they can keep the card regardless of the score on the second ball.
   a. Variations
      i. A player must bowl the value of the card, even if that necessitates throwing a gutter ball on the second throw.
      ii. A player who bowls the desired value on the first throw can earn the card only by converting the spare.
5) If a player, according to the variations selected, bowls the value of the card drawn, then they keep the card.
6) At the end of 10 frames, the player with the most card wins.
7) In the event of a tie, the person with the highest score wins.

Game 15: 9 Pin Knockout

Suggested Level: Advanced

Items Needed: Pen and paper

Object of the Game: Bowl the most consecutive frames with 9 or greater.

Rules:
1) Each Bowler places $1 into the pot to start the game.
2) Each bowler bowls his or her turn.
3) If a bowler knocks down 9 pins or more on his or her first throw, then the bowler's streak continues on the next turn.
4) If a bowler gets less than 9 pins on his or first throw, then they must pay $1 into the pot on the next throw.
5) At the conclusion of the game (or games if the game is a league game or the bowlers decided to play the game for more than one game) the bowler with the longest streak wins.
6) If more than one player has the longest streak, then the players may split the pot or the player with the highest score in the last game will win the pot.
7) Any player failing to place money in the pot after his or streak has been broken, forfeits the ability to win the pot, even if his or her streak was the longest streak.

Game 16: Lucky Roll Race

Suggested Level: Any

Items Needed: Pen, paper, dice, and maybe a calculator

Object of the Game: At the end of the game, whoever earns the most number of steps wins the race and the game.

Rules:
1) Each bowler rolls his or her frame and tries to bowl the highest possible score.
2) The result of the frame results in the before score.
    a. The before score is simply the total number of pins knocked down, except that a strike is worth 11 and a converted split is worth 12 points.
3) After the bowler completes his or her turn, he or she then rolls two dice.
4) The roll of the dice is then subtracted from the before roll score to earn the number of steps.
    a. For example, if a bowler knocks down 9 pins and rolls the dice and gets a 5, then they earn 4 steps.
    b. Negative points can be earned, so if for example, the bowler knocks down 6 pins and rolls a 12, then they take negative 6 steps.
5) In the 10th frame, the dice are rolled two times and total of the two throws is used to determine the dice roll

Example:

Frame	1	2	3	4	5	6	7	8	9	10
Bowler Score	3 /	9 –	X	X	⑦ /	7 2	8 -	9 /	X	5 / x
Before Score	10	9	11	11	12	9	8	10	11	10+11=21
Total Dice Roll	9	5	6	7	7	3	8	12	9	10+8=18
Number of Earned Steps	1	4	5	4	5	6	0	-2	2	3

This player earned a total of 27 steps.

Game 17: Badges

Suggested Level: Any

Items Needed: Pen and paper

Object of the Game: Different bowling combinations or pin counts are set forth ("badges") and whoever can earn the most badges wins. (For example: strike, spare, split, split pick-up, etc.)

Rules:

1) A bowler bowls his or her turn and when the person obtains one of the scores or scoring sequences set forth below, they earn the badge.
2) Only one badge may be earned per turn.
3) A badge may only be earned once.
4) The following are suggested badges:
    a. Strike
    b. Any Spare
    c. 9 Spare
    d. 8 Spare
    e. 7 Spare
    f. 6 Spare
    g. 5 Spare
    h. 4 Spare
    i. 3 Spare
    j. 2 Spare
    k. 1 Spare
    l. Getting the 7-10 Split (not picking it up)
    m. Converting any Split
    n. Strike followed by a Spare
    o. Spare Followed by a Strike
    p. 3 Strikes in Row
5) The game could also be made more interesting by having each bowler contribute a certain amount, say $.50 for each game bowled and the first person to obtain all the badges (or the most for any night) wins the pot.

<u>Note</u>: This game can either be played in one game, i.e. the person to collect the most badges during any game of bowling wins, or, it can be played so that a person to collect all the badges, no matter the number of games bowled, wins. This game can be used a supplemental game for league bowlers, but removing badges f. – k. and perhaps adding a few additional badges.

Game 18: Bingo

Suggested Level: Any

Items Needed: Bingo Cards

Object of the Game: First player to get all the required objectives on the Bingo card chosen by the bowler, all items in a horizontal, vertical or diagonal line wins.

Rules:

1) Determine the following:
   a. Whether one Bingo Card will be used for all Bowlers or whether each Bowler will select his or her own Bingo Card.
   b. Determine whether a player must complete the entire card or just obtain a straight horizontal, diagonal or vertical line composed of 5 consecutive boxes.
   c. Determine if a player must pay to obtain a card.
   d. Determine if players can buy or use more than one card.
   e. Determine the tie breaker:
      i. Player with the highest score at the point of Bingo;
      ii. Player with the most items checked off the Bingo Board;
      iii. The next player to obtain a space on the bingo board
2) As a bowler bowls, they must mark off each item on his or bingo card(s).
3) The first player to obtain the Bingo is the winner.
   a. For various reasons, players who obtain bingo on the same frame, will be considered to have tied.

Bingo cards can be found at the end of this book.

Game 19: Brackets

Suggested Level: Any

Items Needed: Pen and paper, deck of cards

Object of the Game: Beat your opponent head to head and be the only bowler not to lose and you win.

Rules:
This game is a tournament style game of bowling where 2 bowlers will bowl head-to-head for the privilege to advance to the next round. The bowler who wins the final round will be declared the winner. These rules are based on an 8 player bracket and will need to be adjusted based on the number of active participants.

1) Set up a bracket that contains at least 4 bowlers.
    a. If bowlers are bowling this game within a league or a tournament and are bowling 3 games, then the maximum number of bowlers in any bracket is 8.
2) Seed the brackets by placing a number 1-8 on each line of the bracket. Determine the "buy-in", if any, to participate in the tournament.
    a. The "buy-in" will become the pot that the winner of the tournament wins.
3) Determine if any of the bowlers will receive a handicap, and if so what the handicap will be.
4) Pull 1 of each card Ace through 8 from a deck of cards.
5) Shuffle the 8 cards and deal them face down.
6) After paying the buy-in, each bowler draws a card from dealt cards to determine his or her seeding.
    a. For example, the person drawing the Ace will be seeded in the 1 spot on the bracket.
    b. If there are less than 8 bowlers, then any undrawn card can either be a "bye" or assigned an average score. For example, 150.
7) After a game is completed, the player with the highest score wins.
    a. In the event of a tie, tie breakers are as follows:
        i. The bowler with the most strikes;
        ii. The bowler with the most consecutive strikes;
        iii. The bowler with the most split conversions;
        iv. The bowler with the most spares;
        v. The bowler with the least amount of opens; and
        vi. A coin flip.

Example:

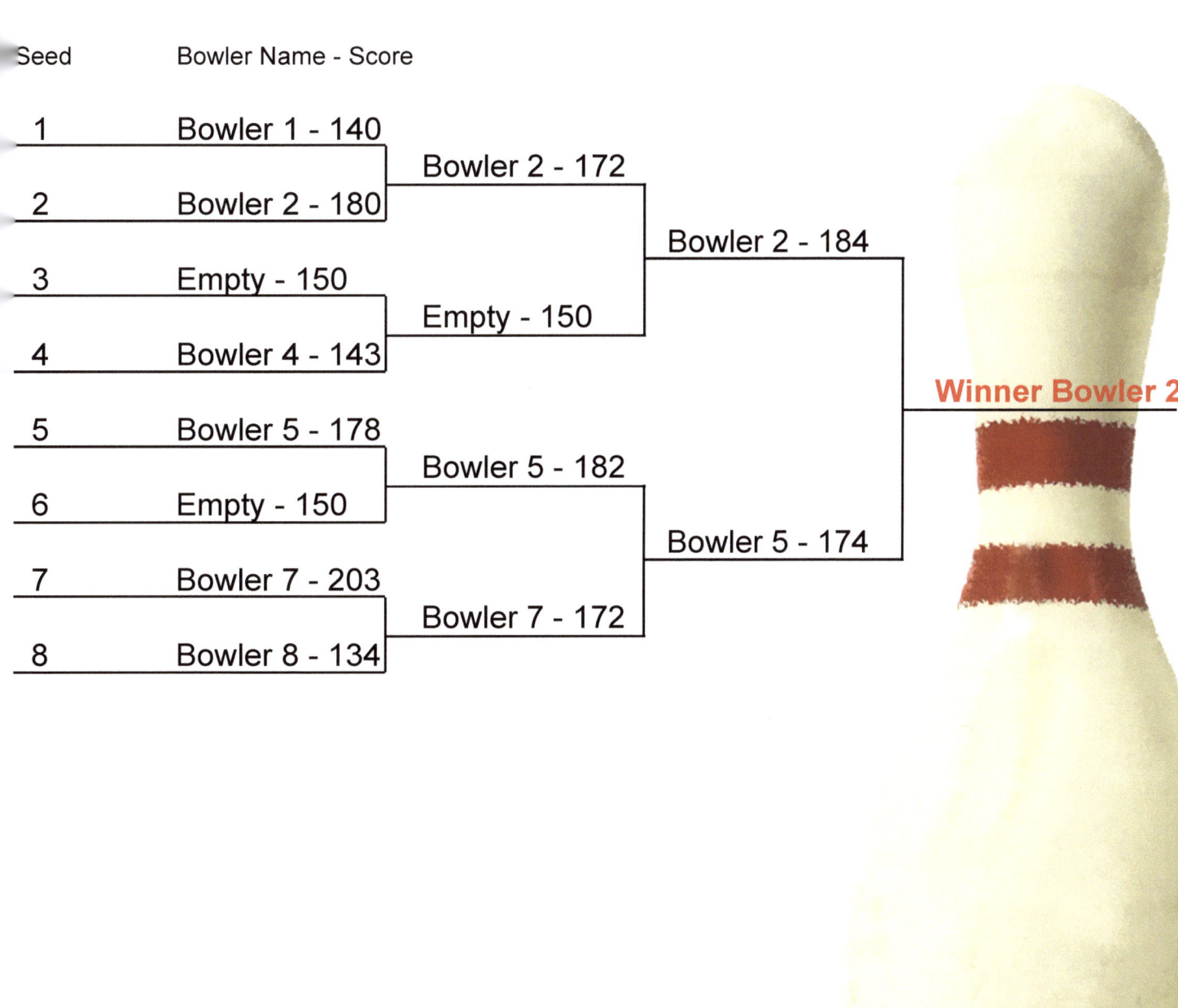

Game 20: BlackJack

Suggested Level: Any

Items Needed: Pen and paper

Object of the Game: To obtain a score in a frame that is evenly divisible by 21. Or in other words, have a frame with a score of: 21, 42, 63, 84, 105, 126, 147, 168, 189, 210, 231, 252, 273, and/or 294.

Rules:

1) Each Bowler places $1 into the pot per frame;
2) Each Bowler tries to obtain a score divisible by 21 in any frame.
3) If a Bowler obtains a score divisible by 21 in a frame where no other bowler has a score evenly divisible by 21, then they win the pot.
    a. A pot cannot be paid out until all bowlers have a score in a frame that requires a payout.
        i. For example, if Bowler one has 42 in the 3rd frame, but Bowler 3 does not yet have a score for the 2nd frame, than the pot for the 3rd frame cannot be paid out until Bowler 3 has a score for the 3rd frame.
4) At the conclusion of the game, the pot either rolls over to the next game, or if the final game has been bowled, then the bowler with the highest bowling score wins the pot.

Card 1

B	I	N	G	O
Split	2 then 2	1 then 5	7 Total Frame	Split Spare
1 then 8	9 First Throw	4 then 5	1 then 1	XX
4 then 2	9 /	FREE SPACE	3 First Throw	6 then 1
7 then 1	4 then 2	3 First Throw	X	1 then 5
2 /	Sleeper	8 Total Frame	8 then 1	1 /

Card 2

B	I	N	G	O
2 then 7	2 then 2	7 - 10 Split	1 then 5	4 then 1
4 First Throw	Sleeper	1 /	5 then 1	3 Total Frame
3 first Throw	3 then 2	FREE SPACE	9 Total Frame	4 then 6
2 Total Frame	4 /	2 First Throw	4 then 4	2 then 5
7 First Throw	8 /	1 then 1	4 then 3	3 then 3

BINGO

B	I	N	G	O
1 /	2 /	1 then 1	3 then 3	3 then 1
3 then 7	Split	5 then 2	2 then 1	2 then 4
4 then 6	4 First Throw	FREE SPACE	1 then 4	5 /
5 Total Frame	X X	1 then 2	2 then 7	Split Spare
8 then 1	4 then 2	4 then 4	2 First Throw	3 First Throw

BINGO

B	I	N	G	O
Big 4	1 then 1	4 First Throw	9 Total Frame	2 then 4
XXXX	3 First Throw	2 then 7	9 /	2 then 2
6 first Throw	2 Total Frame	FREE SPACE	4 then 1	6 then 3
4 then 5	5 then 4	8 First Throw	5 then 3	2 then 6
4 then 6	X	8 /	8 Total Frame	X X

Card 1

BINGO

B	I	N	G	O
3 /	2 /	2 then 4	3 then 4	3 then 1
7 then 2	2 Total Frame	Split	5 /	5 then 1
3 then 4	7 First Throw	FREE SPACE	2 then 5	9 /
XXX	3 Total Frame	2 then 1	5 then 3	1 /
2 then 1	5 then 3	2 then 2	6 First Throw	4 First Throw

BINGO

Card 2

BINGO

B	I	N	G	O
8 /	7 then 1	7 Total Frame	8 then 1	6 Total Frame
9 /	3 Total Frame	2 then 7	5 First Throw	1 First Throw
4 /	7 First Throw	FREE SPACE	3 then 6	6 then 3
5 then 4	5 then 5	Split	5 then 2	2 Total Frame
2 /	4 then 4	7-10 Split	3 then 5	1 then 1

BINGO

Card 1

B I N G O

B	I	N	G	O
4 then 5	3 then 5	8 then 1	XXXX	2 then 2
9 First Throw	4 then 3	5 then 1	8 First Throw	3 then 2
5 /	2 then 1	FREE SPACE	Sleeper	4 Total Frame
3 First Throw	Split Spare	5 Total Frame	8 Total Frame	6 then 2
7 Total Fame	9 Total Fame	3 /	3 then 6	2 then 7

B I N G O

Card 2

B I N G O

B	I	N	G	O
1 then 5	7 then 2	7 - 10 Split	5 then 4	1 then 3
4 then 3	3 First Throw	8 First Throw	1 then 8	1 then 9
5 then 2	5 then 2	FREE SPACE	8 then 1	4 First Throw
2 First Throw	6 then 3	5 Total Frame	1 then 6	2 then 2
1 /	6 Total Frame	3 then 4	9 First Throw	Spare

B I N G O

Copyright © 2014 by Recreational Sports Network, LLC.

All rights reserved. No part of this publication may be reproduced, distributed, or transmitted in any form or by any means, including photocopying, recording, or other electronic or mechanical methods, without the prior written permission of the publisher, except in the case of brief quotations embodied in critical reviews and certain other noncommercial uses permitted by copyright law. For permission requests, write to the publisher, addressed "Attention: Bowling Book," at the address below.

Recreational Sports Network, LLC
P.O. Box 211031
Columbus, Ohio 43221
www.recsportsnetwork.com

-or-

Email: info@recsportsnetwork.com

Ordering Information:
All names of the games contained herein are to be considered trademarks
of Recreational Sports Network, LLC.

Quantity sales. Special discounts are available on quantity purchases by corporations, associations, and others. For details, contact the publisher at the address above.

Printed in the United States of America

ISBN-13: 978-0692251829
First Printing: May 2014

Book Design by Michael Braatz

BOWLING GAMES

www.ingramcontent.com/pod-product-compliance
Lightning Source LLC
LaVergne TN
LVHW072114070426
835510LV00002B/50